DO
EPIC
SHIT
JOURNAL

ANKUR WARIKOO

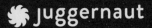

JUGGERNAUT BOOKS
C-I-128, First Floor, Sangam Vihar,
Near Holi Chowk, New Delhi 110080, India

First published by Juggernaut Books 2024

Copyright © Ankur Warikoo 2024

10 9 8 7 6 5 4 3 2 1

ISBN: 9789353456931

All rights reserved. No part of this publication may be reproduced, transmitted, or stored in a retrieval system in any form or by any means without the written permission of the publisher.

Typeset in League Spartan by
R. Ajith Kumar, Noida

Printed at Replika Press Pvt. Ltd.

My monthly habit tracker

MONTH: _____

WORKOUT

① ② ③ ④ ⑤ ⑥ ⑦ ⑧ ⑨ ⑩
⑪ ⑫ ⑬ ⑭ ⑮ ⑯ ⑰ ⑱ ⑲ ⑳
㉑ ㉒ ㉓ ㉔ ㉕ ㉖ ㉗ ㉘ ㉙ ㉚
㉛

READING

① ② ③ ④ ⑤ ⑥ ⑦ ⑧ ⑨ ⑩
⑪ ⑫ ⑬ ⑭ ⑮ ⑯ ⑰ ⑱ ⑲ ⑳
㉑ ㉒ ㉓ ㉔ ㉕ ㉖ ㉗ ㉘ ㉙ ㉚
㉛

5 MINUTES WITH YOURSELF

① ② ③ ④ ⑤ ⑥ ⑦ ⑧ ⑨ ⑩
⑪ ⑫ ⑬ ⑭ ⑮ ⑯ ⑰ ⑱ ⑲ ⑳
㉑ ㉒ ㉓ ㉔ ㉕ ㉖ ㉗ ㉘ ㉙ ㉚
㉛

HEALTHY EATING

① ② ③ ④ ⑤ ⑥ ⑦ ⑧ ⑨ ⑩
⑪ ⑫ ⑬ ⑭ ⑮ ⑯ ⑰ ⑱ ⑲ ⑳
㉑ ㉒ ㉓ ㉔ ㉕ ㉖ ㉗ ㉘ ㉙ ㉚
㉛

7+ HOURS SLEEP

① ② ③ ④ ⑤ ⑥ ⑦ ⑧ ⑨ ⑩
⑪ ⑫ ⑬ ⑭ ⑮ ⑯ ⑰ ⑱ ⑲ ⑳
㉑ ㉒ ㉓ ㉔ ㉕ ㉖ ㉗ ㉘ ㉙ ㉚
㉛

My monthly habit tracker

MONTH: _____

WORKOUT

① ② ③ ④ ⑤ ⑥ ⑦ ⑧ ⑨ ⑩
⑪ ⑫ ⑬ ⑭ ⑮ ⑯ ⑰ ⑱ ⑲ ⑳
㉑ ㉒ ㉓ ㉔ ㉕ ㉖ ㉗ ㉘ ㉙ ㉚
㉛

READING

① ② ③ ④ ⑤ ⑥ ⑦ ⑧ ⑨ ⑩
⑪ ⑫ ⑬ ⑭ ⑮ ⑯ ⑰ ⑱ ⑲ ⑳
㉑ ㉒ ㉓ ㉔ ㉕ ㉖ ㉗ ㉘ ㉙ ㉚
㉛

5 MINUTES WITH YOURSELF

① ② ③ ④ ⑤ ⑥ ⑦ ⑧ ⑨ ⑩
⑪ ⑫ ⑬ ⑭ ⑮ ⑯ ⑰ ⑱ ⑲ ⑳
㉑ ㉒ ㉓ ㉔ ㉕ ㉖ ㉗ ㉘ ㉙ ㉚
㉛

HEALTHY EATING

① ② ③ ④ ⑤ ⑥ ⑦ ⑧ ⑨ ⑩
⑪ ⑫ ⑬ ⑭ ⑮ ⑯ ⑰ ⑱ ⑲ ⑳
㉑ ㉒ ㉓ ㉔ ㉕ ㉖ ㉗ ㉘ ㉙ ㉚
㉛

7+ HOURS SLEEP

① ② ③ ④ ⑤ ⑥ ⑦ ⑧ ⑨ ⑩
⑪ ⑫ ⑬ ⑭ ⑮ ⑯ ⑰ ⑱ ⑲ ⑳
㉑ ㉒ ㉓ ㉔ ㉕ ㉖ ㉗ ㉘ ㉙ ㉚
㉛

My monthly habit tracker

MONTH: _____

WORKOUT

① ② ③ ④ ⑤ ⑥ ⑦ ⑧ ⑨ ⑩
⑪ ⑫ ⑬ ⑭ ⑮ ⑯ ⑰ ⑱ ⑲ ⑳
㉑ ㉒ ㉓ ㉔ ㉕ ㉖ ㉗ ㉘ ㉙ ㉚
㉛

READING

① ② ③ ④ ⑤ ⑥ ⑦ ⑧ ⑨ ⑩
⑪ ⑫ ⑬ ⑭ ⑮ ⑯ ⑰ ⑱ ⑲ ⑳
㉑ ㉒ ㉓ ㉔ ㉕ ㉖ ㉗ ㉘ ㉙ ㉚
㉛

5 MINUTES WITH YOURSELF

① ② ③ ④ ⑤ ⑥ ⑦ ⑧ ⑨ ⑩
⑪ ⑫ ⑬ ⑭ ⑮ ⑯ ⑰ ⑱ ⑲ ⑳
㉑ ㉒ ㉓ ㉔ ㉕ ㉖ ㉗ ㉘ ㉙ ㉚
㉛

HEALTHY EATING

① ② ③ ④ ⑤ ⑥ ⑦ ⑧ ⑨ ⑩
⑪ ⑫ ⑬ ⑭ ⑮ ⑯ ⑰ ⑱ ⑲ ⑳
㉑ ㉒ ㉓ ㉔ ㉕ ㉖ ㉗ ㉘ ㉙ ㉚
㉛

7+ HOURS SLEEP

① ② ③ ④ ⑤ ⑥ ⑦ ⑧ ⑨ ⑩
⑪ ⑫ ⑬ ⑭ ⑮ ⑯ ⑰ ⑱ ⑲ ⑳
㉑ ㉒ ㉓ ㉔ ㉕ ㉖ ㉗ ㉘ ㉙ ㉚
㉛

My monthly habit tracker

MONTH: _____

WORKOUT

① ② ③ ④ ⑤ ⑥ ⑦ ⑧ ⑨ ⑩
⑪ ⑫ ⑬ ⑭ ⑮ ⑯ ⑰ ⑱ ⑲ ⑳
㉑ ㉒ ㉓ ㉔ ㉕ ㉖ ㉗ ㉘ ㉙ ㉚
㉛

READING

① ② ③ ④ ⑤ ⑥ ⑦ ⑧ ⑨ ⑩
⑪ ⑫ ⑬ ⑭ ⑮ ⑯ ⑰ ⑱ ⑲ ⑳
㉑ ㉒ ㉓ ㉔ ㉕ ㉖ ㉗ ㉘ ㉙ ㉚
㉛

5 MINUTES WITH YOURSELF

① ② ③ ④ ⑤ ⑥ ⑦ ⑧ ⑨ ⑩
⑪ ⑫ ⑬ ⑭ ⑮ ⑯ ⑰ ⑱ ⑲ ⑳
㉑ ㉒ ㉓ ㉔ ㉕ ㉖ ㉗ ㉘ ㉙ ㉚
㉛

HEALTHY EATING

① ② ③ ④ ⑤ ⑥ ⑦ ⑧ ⑨ ⑩
⑪ ⑫ ⑬ ⑭ ⑮ ⑯ ⑰ ⑱ ⑲ ⑳
㉑ ㉒ ㉓ ㉔ ㉕ ㉖ ㉗ ㉘ ㉙ ㉚
㉛

7+ HOURS SLEEP

① ② ③ ④ ⑤ ⑥ ⑦ ⑧ ⑨ ⑩
⑪ ⑫ ⑬ ⑭ ⑮ ⑯ ⑰ ⑱ ⑲ ⑳
㉑ ㉒ ㉓ ㉔ ㉕ ㉖ ㉗ ㉘ ㉙ ㉚
㉛

My monthly habit tracker

MONTH: _____

WORKOUT

① ② ③ ④ ⑤ ⑥ ⑦ ⑧ ⑨ ⑩
⑪ ⑫ ⑬ ⑭ ⑮ ⑯ ⑰ ⑱ ⑲ ⑳
㉑ ㉒ ㉓ ㉔ ㉕ ㉖ ㉗ ㉘ ㉙ ㉚
㉛

READING

① ② ③ ④ ⑤ ⑥ ⑦ ⑧ ⑨ ⑩
⑪ ⑫ ⑬ ⑭ ⑮ ⑯ ⑰ ⑱ ⑲ ⑳
㉑ ㉒ ㉓ ㉔ ㉕ ㉖ ㉗ ㉘ ㉙ ㉚
㉛

5 MINUTES WITH YOURSELF

① ② ③ ④ ⑤ ⑥ ⑦ ⑧ ⑨ ⑩
⑪ ⑫ ⑬ ⑭ ⑮ ⑯ ⑰ ⑱ ⑲ ⑳
㉑ ㉒ ㉓ ㉔ ㉕ ㉖ ㉗ ㉘ ㉙ ㉚
㉛

HEALTHY EATING

① ② ③ ④ ⑤ ⑥ ⑦ ⑧ ⑨ ⑩
⑪ ⑫ ⑬ ⑭ ⑮ ⑯ ⑰ ⑱ ⑲ ⑳
㉑ ㉒ ㉓ ㉔ ㉕ ㉖ ㉗ ㉘ ㉙ ㉚
㉛

7+ HOURS SLEEP

① ② ③ ④ ⑤ ⑥ ⑦ ⑧ ⑨ ⑩
⑪ ⑫ ⑬ ⑭ ⑮ ⑯ ⑰ ⑱ ⑲ ⑳
㉑ ㉒ ㉓ ㉔ ㉕ ㉖ ㉗ ㉘ ㉙ ㉚
㉛

My monthly habit tracker

MONTH: _____

WORKOUT

① ② ③ ④ ⑤ ⑥ ⑦ ⑧ ⑨ ⑩
⑪ ⑫ ⑬ ⑭ ⑮ ⑯ ⑰ ⑱ ⑲ ⑳
㉑ ㉒ ㉓ ㉔ ㉕ ㉖ ㉗ ㉘ ㉙ ㉚
㉛

READING

① ② ③ ④ ⑤ ⑥ ⑦ ⑧ ⑨ ⑩
⑪ ⑫ ⑬ ⑭ ⑮ ⑯ ⑰ ⑱ ⑲ ⑳
㉑ ㉒ ㉓ ㉔ ㉕ ㉖ ㉗ ㉘ ㉙ ㉚
㉛

5 MINUTES WITH YOURSELF

① ② ③ ④ ⑤ ⑥ ⑦ ⑧ ⑨ ⑩
⑪ ⑫ ⑬ ⑭ ⑮ ⑯ ⑰ ⑱ ⑲ ⑳
㉑ ㉒ ㉓ ㉔ ㉕ ㉖ ㉗ ㉘ ㉙ ㉚
㉛

HEALTHY EATING

① ② ③ ④ ⑤ ⑥ ⑦ ⑧ ⑨ ⑩
⑪ ⑫ ⑬ ⑭ ⑮ ⑯ ⑰ ⑱ ⑲ ⑳
㉑ ㉒ ㉓ ㉔ ㉕ ㉖ ㉗ ㉘ ㉙ ㉚
㉛

7+ HOURS SLEEP

① ② ③ ④ ⑤ ⑥ ⑦ ⑧ ⑨ ⑩
⑪ ⑫ ⑬ ⑭ ⑮ ⑯ ⑰ ⑱ ⑲ ⑳
㉑ ㉒ ㉓ ㉔ ㉕ ㉖ ㉗ ㉘ ㉙ ㉚
㉛

My monthly habit tracker

MONTH: _____

WORKOUT

① ② ③ ④ ⑤ ⑥ ⑦ ⑧ ⑨ ⑩
⑪ ⑫ ⑬ ⑭ ⑮ ⑯ ⑰ ⑱ ⑲ ⑳
㉑ ㉒ ㉓ ㉔ ㉕ ㉖ ㉗ ㉘ ㉙ ㉚
㉛

READING

① ② ③ ④ ⑤ ⑥ ⑦ ⑧ ⑨ ⑩
⑪ ⑫ ⑬ ⑭ ⑮ ⑯ ⑰ ⑱ ⑲ ⑳
㉑ ㉒ ㉓ ㉔ ㉕ ㉖ ㉗ ㉘ ㉙ ㉚
㉛

5 MINUTES WITH YOURSELF

① ② ③ ④ ⑤ ⑥ ⑦ ⑧ ⑨ ⑩
⑪ ⑫ ⑬ ⑭ ⑮ ⑯ ⑰ ⑱ ⑲ ⑳
㉑ ㉒ ㉓ ㉔ ㉕ ㉖ ㉗ ㉘ ㉙ ㉚
㉛

HEALTHY EATING

① ② ③ ④ ⑤ ⑥ ⑦ ⑧ ⑨ ⑩
⑪ ⑫ ⑬ ⑭ ⑮ ⑯ ⑰ ⑱ ⑲ ⑳
㉑ ㉒ ㉓ ㉔ ㉕ ㉖ ㉗ ㉘ ㉙ ㉚
㉛

7+ HOURS SLEEP

① ② ③ ④ ⑤ ⑥ ⑦ ⑧ ⑨ ⑩
⑪ ⑫ ⑬ ⑭ ⑮ ⑯ ⑰ ⑱ ⑲ ⑳
㉑ ㉒ ㉓ ㉔ ㉕ ㉖ ㉗ ㉘ ㉙ ㉚
㉛

My monthly habit tracker

MONTH: _____

WORKOUT

① ② ③ ④ ⑤ ⑥ ⑦ ⑧ ⑨ ⑩
⑪ ⑫ ⑬ ⑭ ⑮ ⑯ ⑰ ⑱ ⑲ ⑳
㉑ ㉒ ㉓ ㉔ ㉕ ㉖ ㉗ ㉘ ㉙ ㉚
㉛

READING

① ② ③ ④ ⑤ ⑥ ⑦ ⑧ ⑨ ⑩
⑪ ⑫ ⑬ ⑭ ⑮ ⑯ ⑰ ⑱ ⑲ ⑳
㉑ ㉒ ㉓ ㉔ ㉕ ㉖ ㉗ ㉘ ㉙ ㉚
㉛

5 MINUTES WITH YOURSELF

① ② ③ ④ ⑤ ⑥ ⑦ ⑧ ⑨ ⑩
⑪ ⑫ ⑬ ⑭ ⑮ ⑯ ⑰ ⑱ ⑲ ⑳
㉑ ㉒ ㉓ ㉔ ㉕ ㉖ ㉗ ㉘ ㉙ ㉚
㉛

HEALTHY EATING

① ② ③ ④ ⑤ ⑥ ⑦ ⑧ ⑨ ⑩
⑪ ⑫ ⑬ ⑭ ⑮ ⑯ ⑰ ⑱ ⑲ ⑳
㉑ ㉒ ㉓ ㉔ ㉕ ㉖ ㉗ ㉘ ㉙ ㉚
㉛

7+ HOURS SLEEP

① ② ③ ④ ⑤ ⑥ ⑦ ⑧ ⑨ ⑩
⑪ ⑫ ⑬ ⑭ ⑮ ⑯ ⑰ ⑱ ⑲ ⑳
㉑ ㉒ ㉓ ㉔ ㉕ ㉖ ㉗ ㉘ ㉙ ㉚
㉛

My monthly habit tracker

MONTH: _____

WORKOUT

① ② ③ ④ ⑤ ⑥ ⑦ ⑧ ⑨ ⑩
⑪ ⑫ ⑬ ⑭ ⑮ ⑯ ⑰ ⑱ ⑲ ⑳
㉑ ㉒ ㉓ ㉔ ㉕ ㉖ ㉗ ㉘ ㉙ ㉚
㉛

READING

① ② ③ ④ ⑤ ⑥ ⑦ ⑧ ⑨ ⑩
⑪ ⑫ ⑬ ⑭ ⑮ ⑯ ⑰ ⑱ ⑲ ⑳
㉑ ㉒ ㉓ ㉔ ㉕ ㉖ ㉗ ㉘ ㉙ ㉚
㉛

5 MINUTES WITH YOURSELF

① ② ③ ④ ⑤ ⑥ ⑦ ⑧ ⑨ ⑩
⑪ ⑫ ⑬ ⑭ ⑮ ⑯ ⑰ ⑱ ⑲ ⑳
㉑ ㉒ ㉓ ㉔ ㉕ ㉖ ㉗ ㉘ ㉙ ㉚
㉛

HEALTHY EATING

① ② ③ ④ ⑤ ⑥ ⑦ ⑧ ⑨ ⑩
⑪ ⑫ ⑬ ⑭ ⑮ ⑯ ⑰ ⑱ ⑲ ⑳
㉑ ㉒ ㉓ ㉔ ㉕ ㉖ ㉗ ㉘ ㉙ ㉚
㉛

7+ HOURS SLEEP

① ② ③ ④ ⑤ ⑥ ⑦ ⑧ ⑨ ⑩
⑪ ⑫ ⑬ ⑭ ⑮ ⑯ ⑰ ⑱ ⑲ ⑳
㉑ ㉒ ㉓ ㉔ ㉕ ㉖ ㉗ ㉘ ㉙ ㉚
㉛

My monthly habit tracker

MONTH: _____

WORKOUT

① ② ③ ④ ⑤ ⑥ ⑦ ⑧ ⑨ ⑩
⑪ ⑫ ⑬ ⑭ ⑮ ⑯ ⑰ ⑱ ⑲ ⑳
㉑ ㉒ ㉓ ㉔ ㉕ ㉖ ㉗ ㉘ ㉙ ㉚
㉛

READING

① ② ③ ④ ⑤ ⑥ ⑦ ⑧ ⑨ ⑩
⑪ ⑫ ⑬ ⑭ ⑮ ⑯ ⑰ ⑱ ⑲ ⑳
㉑ ㉒ ㉓ ㉔ ㉕ ㉖ ㉗ ㉘ ㉙ ㉚
㉛

5 MINUTES WITH YOURSELF

① ② ③ ④ ⑤ ⑥ ⑦ ⑧ ⑨ ⑩
⑪ ⑫ ⑬ ⑭ ⑮ ⑯ ⑰ ⑱ ⑲ ⑳
㉑ ㉒ ㉓ ㉔ ㉕ ㉖ ㉗ ㉘ ㉙ ㉚
㉛

HEALTHY EATING

① ② ③ ④ ⑤ ⑥ ⑦ ⑧ ⑨ ⑩
⑪ ⑫ ⑬ ⑭ ⑮ ⑯ ⑰ ⑱ ⑲ ⑳
㉑ ㉒ ㉓ ㉔ ㉕ ㉖ ㉗ ㉘ ㉙ ㉚
㉛

7+ HOURS SLEEP

① ② ③ ④ ⑤ ⑥ ⑦ ⑧ ⑨ ⑩
⑪ ⑫ ⑬ ⑭ ⑮ ⑯ ⑰ ⑱ ⑲ ⑳
㉑ ㉒ ㉓ ㉔ ㉕ ㉖ ㉗ ㉘ ㉙ ㉚
㉛

My monthly habit tracker

MONTH: _____

WORKOUT

① ② ③ ④ ⑤ ⑥ ⑦ ⑧ ⑨ ⑩
⑪ ⑫ ⑬ ⑭ ⑮ ⑯ ⑰ ⑱ ⑲ ⑳
㉑ ㉒ ㉓ ㉔ ㉕ ㉖ ㉗ ㉘ ㉙ ㉚
㉛

READING

① ② ③ ④ ⑤ ⑥ ⑦ ⑧ ⑨ ⑩
⑪ ⑫ ⑬ ⑭ ⑮ ⑯ ⑰ ⑱ ⑲ ⑳
㉑ ㉒ ㉓ ㉔ ㉕ ㉖ ㉗ ㉘ ㉙ ㉚
㉛

5 MINUTES WITH YOURSELF

① ② ③ ④ ⑤ ⑥ ⑦ ⑧ ⑨ ⑩
⑪ ⑫ ⑬ ⑭ ⑮ ⑯ ⑰ ⑱ ⑲ ⑳
㉑ ㉒ ㉓ ㉔ ㉕ ㉖ ㉗ ㉘ ㉙ ㉚
㉛

HEALTHY EATING

① ② ③ ④ ⑤ ⑥ ⑦ ⑧ ⑨ ⑩
⑪ ⑫ ⑬ ⑭ ⑮ ⑯ ⑰ ⑱ ⑲ ⑳
㉑ ㉒ ㉓ ㉔ ㉕ ㉖ ㉗ ㉘ ㉙ ㉚
㉛

7+ HOURS SLEEP

① ② ③ ④ ⑤ ⑥ ⑦ ⑧ ⑨ ⑩
⑪ ⑫ ⑬ ⑭ ⑮ ⑯ ⑰ ⑱ ⑲ ⑳
㉑ ㉒ ㉓ ㉔ ㉕ ㉖ ㉗ ㉘ ㉙ ㉚
㉛

My monthly habit tracker

MONTH: _____

WORKOUT

① ② ③ ④ ⑤ ⑥ ⑦ ⑧ ⑨ ⑩
⑪ ⑫ ⑬ ⑭ ⑮ ⑯ ⑰ ⑱ ⑲ ⑳
㉑ ㉒ ㉓ ㉔ ㉕ ㉖ ㉗ ㉘ ㉙ ㉚
㉛

READING

① ② ③ ④ ⑤ ⑥ ⑦ ⑧ ⑨ ⑩
⑪ ⑫ ⑬ ⑭ ⑮ ⑯ ⑰ ⑱ ⑲ ⑳
㉑ ㉒ ㉓ ㉔ ㉕ ㉖ ㉗ ㉘ ㉙ ㉚
㉛

5 MINUTES WITH YOURSELF

① ② ③ ④ ⑤ ⑥ ⑦ ⑧ ⑨ ⑩
⑪ ⑫ ⑬ ⑭ ⑮ ⑯ ⑰ ⑱ ⑲ ⑳
㉑ ㉒ ㉓ ㉔ ㉕ ㉖ ㉗ ㉘ ㉙ ㉚
㉛

HEALTHY EATING

① ② ③ ④ ⑤ ⑥ ⑦ ⑧ ⑨ ⑩
⑪ ⑫ ⑬ ⑭ ⑮ ⑯ ⑰ ⑱ ⑲ ⑳
㉑ ㉒ ㉓ ㉔ ㉕ ㉖ ㉗ ㉘ ㉙ ㉚
㉛

7+ HOURS SLEEP

① ② ③ ④ ⑤ ⑥ ⑦ ⑧ ⑨ ⑩
⑪ ⑫ ⑬ ⑭ ⑮ ⑯ ⑰ ⑱ ⑲ ⑳
㉑ ㉒ ㉓ ㉔ ㉕ ㉖ ㉗ ㉘ ㉙ ㉚
㉛

A year from now, you will wish you had started today. Start today.

Nothing beats the feeling of having done more in twenty-four hours than what the day expected you to!

How we think of our problems is how the world will think of our problems.

You are what you do.
Not what you say you'll do.

Others' success will generate massive self-doubt every morning when you get up. Get up anyway.

What is the single biggest thing you can do to help you towards professional success?

People do not have to follow up when you commit to doing something. That's it.

My Sunday page

DATE: /   /

TOP 3 THINGS I DID THIS WEEK

✓ ....
....
....
....

✓ ....
....
....
....

✓ ....
....
....
....

THIS WEEK I FELT

HOW I WOULD RATE MYSELF THIS WEEK
☆ ☆ ☆ ☆ ☆

THE BEST THING THAT HAPPENED TO ME THIS WEEK

....
....
....
....
....
....
....

WHAT I WANT TO DO NEXT WEEK

....
....
....
....
....
....
....

It is the story in your head that is the most important story. Always remember that.

Luck happens to those that make things happen.

**Persistence isn't a one-day miracle.
It is a conscious choice translated into habit.**

We have just one life.

Why live it with just one identity?

Serendipity happens to those who are not married to the outcome. Instead, to the process.

The biggest misconception people have is that they are the odd one out and everyone else is sorted!

The world will constantly be defining success and failure for you. Realizing this is what is called self-awareness.

My Sunday page

DATE: / /

TOP 3 THINGS I DID THIS WEEK

✓ ....
....
....
....

✓ ....
....
....
....

✓ ....
....
....
....

THE BEST THING THAT HAPPENED TO ME THIS WEEK

....
....
....
....
....
....
....
....
....
....
....

WHAT I WANT TO DO NEXT WEEK

....
....
....
....
....
....
....
....
....

THIS WEEK I FELT

😀 🙂 😐 🙁 ☹️ 😫
😊 😕 😠 😜 😶

HOW I WOULD RATE MYSELF THIS WEEK

☆ ☆ ☆ ☆ ☆

If you are unhappy with where you are in life right now, do not wait to find out what you should be doing.

Move out of where you are in life!

The pro is the amateur who simply showed up every day.

Even when you know things may never be the same again, apologize.

Because you should.

Don't measure how valuable you are by the way you are treated.

Whatever you are feeling today will fade away.

Most sports are not played on the field.

They are played in the mind!

My Sunday page

DATE: /   /

TOP 3 THINGS I DID THIS WEEK

✓

✓

✓

THIS WEEK I FELT

HOW I WOULD RATE MYSELF THIS WEEK
☆ ☆ ☆ ☆ ☆

THE BEST THING THAT HAPPENED TO ME THIS WEEK

WHAT I WANT TO DO NEXT WEEK

The biggest roadblock to learning is ego!

When you say you have five years of experience, is it five years of experience or one year of experience done five times over?

Finding a mentor is a journey everyone should embark upon.

Movement brings momentum. Stagnation amplifies sadness.

You don't find your passion. You grow your passion!

We were ALL born with the innate ability to ask questions. Endlessly.

My Sunday page

DATE: /   /

TOP 3 THINGS I DID THIS WEEK

✓ ....
....
....
....

✓ ....
....
....
....

✓ ....
....
....
....

THIS WEEK I FELT

HOW I WOULD RATE MYSELF THIS WEEK

☆ ☆ ☆ ☆ ☆

THE BEST THING THAT HAPPENED TO ME THIS WEEK

....
....
....
....
....
....
....
....

WHAT I WANT TO DO NEXT WEEK

....
....
....
....
....
....
....
....

**Once you succeed, people see only success.
If you fail, they see only failure.**

They don't see the journey. Only you do. It is on this journey that your life was lived!

If you often worry about what people will think of you, you will often end up doing what people want you to do.

3 relationships that define almost everything that happens to us in our lives.

- **The relationship we have with money.**
- **The relationship we have with time.**
- **The relationship we have with ourselves.**

Fighting the stereotype is a great way to get attention!

There is temporary discomfort in doing the unconventional.

While you are building your skills, the most important thing to build is your reputation.

Your goal is to make people say: 'I am not sure if she knows how to do it. But I am certain if told to do it, she will definitely figure it out. I trust her.'

My Sunday page

DATE: /   /

TOP 3 THINGS I DID THIS WEEK

✓
....
....
....
....

✓
....
....
....
....

✓
....
....
....
....

THIS WEEK I FELT

HOW I WOULD RATE MYSELF THIS WEEK

☆ ☆ ☆ ☆ ☆

THE BEST THING THAT HAPPENED TO ME THIS WEEK

....
....
....
....
....
....
....

WHAT I WANT TO DO NEXT WEEK

....
....
....
....
....
....
....
....

The best relationships have the best acceptances despite their differences.

The trick to waking up early is not waking up early. It is sleeping on time!

We accept the love we think we deserve.

The day we start loving ourselves, we raise the bar for the one we fall in love with.

Share your journey. Document your journey. Narrate your journey.

Curiosity has created more opportunities than hard work ever will.

Targets are the enemy of habits.

Don't set targets. Set habits!

**Don't try to minimize your struggle.
Try to make it more meaningful.**

My Sunday page

DATE: /   /

TOP 3 THINGS I DID THIS WEEK

✓ ....

✓ ....

✓ ....

THIS WEEK I FELT

HOW I WOULD RATE MYSELF THIS WEEK

☆ ☆ ☆ ☆ ☆

THE BEST THING THAT HAPPENED TO ME THIS WEEK

WHAT I WANT TO DO NEXT WEEK

Before you assume, try this crazy thing. ASK!

You won't get out of laziness for something you don't want to do.

Most important skills today that are hardly taught: Humour, storytelling, managing money, human psychology and cold emailing.

To start the habit of reading books, read books that you will enjoy.

Not books that the world thinks you should be reading!

The best form of writing is the one that is written neither out of fear nor with the willingness to share.

Three things that will tell you who/what you consider important in your life.

1. Your first hour after you wake up
2. Your last hour before you sleep
3. Your calendar

My Sunday page

DATE: / /

TOP 3 THINGS I DID THIS WEEK

✓ ....

....

....

....

✓ ....

....

....

....

✓ ....

....

....

....

THIS WEEK I FELT

HOW I WOULD RATE MYSELF THIS WEEK

☆ ☆ ☆ ☆ ☆

THE BEST THING THAT HAPPENED TO ME THIS WEEK

....

....

....

....

....

....

....

....

....

....

WHAT I WANT TO DO NEXT WEEK

....

....

....

....

....

....

....

....

We are shaped by the stories we tell ourselves.

We know others through their actions.
We know ourselves through our thoughts.

Daily progress isn't about becoming an expert in your field. It is developing the mindset that progress is a way of life. It is like breathing. We rarely stop to acknowledge it. But we breathe every second. We would die without it.

**We nod to show that we are listening.
But we are not listening to the opposite person.
Instead, we are listening to our mind telling us
what to say.**

**Your attendance doesn't define your discipline.
Your attention does.**

Optimize for learning, not salary.
Optimize for progress, not stability.
Optimize for facing fears, not for comfort.

My Sunday page

DATE: / /

TOP 3 THINGS I DID THIS WEEK

✓ ....
....
....
....

✓ ....
....
....
....

✓ ....
....
....
....

THIS WEEK I FELT

HOW I WOULD RATE MYSELF THIS WEEK

☆ ☆ ☆ ☆ ☆

THE BEST THING THAT HAPPENED TO ME THIS WEEK

....
....
....
....
....
....
....

WHAT I WANT TO DO NEXT WEEK

....
....
....
....
....
....
....
....

Who you spend time with will define the stories you hear. The stories you hear will define the stories in your head. The stories in your head will define you. Choose who you spend time with, wisely!

Some of the smartest people in the world are competing for your sleep time.

Do not allow comfort to make you believe that you no longer need to try!

In a society that is obsessed with hard work and career success, seeking boredom is an act of rebellion.

If you follow the right set of people on social media, opportunities will come by design. Not by luck!

If everyone did it, it wouldn't need to be said.

My Sunday page

DATE: /   /

TOP 3 THINGS I DID THIS WEEK

✓ ....
....
....
....

✓ ....
....
....
....

✓ ....
....
....

THIS WEEK I FELT

HOW I WOULD RATE MYSELF THIS WEEK

☆ ☆ ☆ ☆

THE BEST THING THAT HAPPENED TO ME THIS WEEK

....
....
....
....
....
....
....
....

WHAT I WANT TO DO NEXT WEEK

....
....
....
....
....
....
....
....

Run away from those who never run towards themselves.

No step is small, as long as it is headed in the direction of where we want to go.

Most of my decisions in life were not made because of my confidence in the decision.

They were made because of my awareness of the situation.

Our actions are driven by our feeling of what people feel about us!

This begs the question, whose life are we living?

Find it hard to say 'no' to people, when you know you should?

It's mostly because you worry about what they will think of you.

Emotional debt has killed more people than financial debt ever will.

If unsure between two choices, picking both is almost always the wrong response.

My Sunday page

DATE: /   /

TOP 3 THINGS I DID THIS WEEK

✓ ....

✓ ....

✓ ....

THE BEST THING THAT HAPPENED TO ME THIS WEEK

WHAT I WANT TO DO NEXT WEEK

THIS WEEK I FELT

HOW I WOULD RATE MYSELF THIS WEEK

☆ ☆ ☆ ☆ ☆

Being calm is a skill.

Fear has led to more procrastination than laziness ever will.

Just because someone carries it well doesn't mean it isn't heavy. Everyone carries a heavy load. Be kind to others.

Finding security in your own achievement is the biggest achievement.

Do not confuse calmness with a lack of fire.

Your self-talk determines your self-worth.

My Sunday page

DATE: /   /

TOP 3 THINGS I DID THIS WEEK

✓

✓

✓

THIS WEEK I FELT

HOW I WOULD RATE MYSELF THIS WEEK

☆ ☆ ☆ ☆ ☆

THE BEST THING THAT HAPPENED TO ME THIS WEEK

WHAT I WANT TO DO NEXT WEEK

Not making a decision because you are scared of making the wrong decision?

If you don't move, you would've already made the wrong decision.

Who is the person you would disappoint the most if you failed?

What if you free yourself from the fear of letting them down?

If you are not having fun while doing it, people will see through it.

That thing that you still haven't finished and you are mad at yourself for not doing so?

It is simply because it is not a priority. You think you still have time.

The second we think decisions are reversible, we start giving serendipity a chance!

Knowing when to say no and saying it is a life skill.

My Sunday page

DATE: /   /

TOP 3 THINGS I DID THIS WEEK

✓

✓

✓

THIS WEEK I FELT

HOW I WOULD RATE MYSELF THIS WEEK

☆ ☆ ☆ ☆

THE BEST THING THAT HAPPENED TO ME THIS WEEK

WHAT I WANT TO DO NEXT WEEK

Merely knowing what you need to do is not enough for you to do it!

Awareness is the start of the decision. Not the end of it.

If you are authentic, if you are truly yourself all the time – you don't have any competition!

No one can ever beat you at being you!

It is better to be busy in the chase of finding yourself instead of being busy in the rat race and never knowing yourself.

Comparing yourself to others is the biggest waste of time.

We always have two choices:

1. The easy one

2. The right one

**We aren't addicted to things.
We are addicted to the emotions that these things generate!**

My Sunday page

DATE: /   /

TOP 3 THINGS I DID THIS WEEK

✓ ....
....
....
....

✓ ....
....
....
....

✓ ....
....
....
....

THE BEST THING THAT HAPPENED TO ME THIS WEEK

....
....
....
....
....
....
....

WHAT I WANT TO DO NEXT WEEK

....
....
....
....
....
....
....
....

THIS WEEK I FELT

HOW I WOULD RATE MYSELF THIS WEEK

☆ ☆ ☆ ☆ ☆

Truth, as scary and scarry as it is, comes with the courage to speak up. And stand by it.

Don't go to college just looking for a job, a title, a company, a function, a role, a salary.

Go to college looking for yourself.

If you don't ask, the answer is always no.

We always have choices.
No one's ever stuck.
We are just scared to make those choices.

You don't control what the world says about you.

You control what YOU say when the world says something about you.

Spent years doing something that you do not enjoy any more?

Think of the time that lies ahead, not of the time that lies in the past!

The most dangerous people in the world are not the ones who are ignorant.

They are the ones who are ignorant but BELIEVE they are right!

My Sunday page

DATE: /   /

TOP 3 THINGS I DID THIS WEEK

✓ ....
....
....
....

✓ ....
....
....
....

✓ ....
....
....
....

THIS WEEK I FELT

HOW I WOULD RATE MYSELF THIS WEEK
☆ ☆ ☆ ☆ ☆

THE BEST THING THAT HAPPENED TO ME THIS WEEK

....
....
....
....
....
....
....
....

WHAT I WANT TO DO NEXT WEEK

....
....
....
....
....
....
....
....

People will help you only when you have helped them understand how they can.

The distance between 'I could have' and 'I have' is regret.

The hardest thing in the world is telling yourself that it's not hard at all.

If you are scared of losing, you have already lost!

The most memorable moments of your life would have a sense of freedom attached to them.

Instead of worrying about what might happen, anticipate what might happen.

My Sunday page

DATE: /   /

TOP 3 THINGS I DID THIS WEEK

✓

✓

✓

THIS WEEK I FELT

HOW I WOULD RATE MYSELF THIS WEEK

☆ ☆ ☆ ☆

THE BEST THING THAT HAPPENED TO ME THIS WEEK

WHAT I WANT TO DO NEXT WEEK

Life is full of struggle.

A corporate job can be a great start to a career.

Do not mistake starting slow as starting small.

Everyone is struggling.
Everyone is figuring it out.

Don't be harsh on yourself.

When it comes to money, more information doesn't make people more aware.

It makes them more scared.

Being grateful in life for what you have is precious.

My Sunday page

DATE: / /

TOP 3 THINGS I DID THIS WEEK

✓

✓

✓

THE BEST THING THAT HAPPENED TO ME THIS WEEK

THIS WEEK I FELT

WHAT I WANT TO DO NEXT WEEK

HOW I WOULD RATE MYSELF THIS WEEK

☆ ☆ ☆ ☆ ☆

The greatest illusion is that life should be perfect!

As adults, the single biggest hurdle to learning is pride!

People who are enjoying their lives are at a competitive advantage.

If you didn't say it earlier, don't say it during your exit interview.

A meaningful job need not be one that completely consumes your whole life.

To not have a plan and be okay with it is the best plan. It will take everything to get to that point.

My Sunday page

DATE: /   /

TOP 3 THINGS I DID THIS WEEK

✓ ....

....

....

....

✓ ....

....

....

....

✓ ....

....

....

....

THIS WEEK I FELT

HOW I WOULD RATE MYSELF THIS WEEK

☆ ☆ ☆ ☆ ☆

THE BEST THING THAT HAPPENED TO ME THIS WEEK

....

....

....

....

....

....

....

....

....

WHAT I WANT TO DO NEXT WEEK

....

....

....

....

....

....

....

Knowing that you don't know much, is the best knowledge.

If you are comfortable dancing in public without alcohol or drugs, you are at peace with who you are.

**The easiest way to learn from mistakes is to read books.
The next option is to commit them yourself.**

Resisting the obvious is a great way to change your orbit. If you do what everyone else will do, you will end up like everyone else.

Complaining has never ever led someone to a solution.

Working out teaches you discipline and patience like few other things do.

How you treat someone who has nothing to offer defines your value system.

Your values don't help you grow.

But in times of shit, they hold you together.

My Sunday page

DATE: /   /

TOP 3 THINGS I DID THIS WEEK

✓ ....
....
....
....

✓ ....
....
....
....

✓ ....
....
....
....

THIS WEEK I FELT

HOW I WOULD RATE MYSELF THIS WEEK

☆ ☆ ☆ ☆

THE BEST THING THAT HAPPENED TO ME THIS WEEK

....
....
....
....
....
....
....
....

WHAT I WANT TO DO NEXT WEEK

....
....
....
....
....
....
....
....

Don't ever fool yourself to believe you deserve to be where you are in life.

You will get what you seek.

Telling someone they are wrong is never going to convince the person.

People would much rather work for a competent asshole than an incompetent nice guy.

Capability is rarely the question mark in life. It is always the intent.

Telling someone you will never understand is you facing the mirror.

My Sunday page

DATE: /   /

TOP 3 THINGS I DID THIS WEEK

✓ ....

....

....

✓ ....

....

....

✓ ....

....

....

THE BEST THING THAT HAPPENED TO ME THIS WEEK

....
....
....
....
....
....

WHAT I WANT TO DO NEXT WEEK

....
....
....
....
....
....

THIS WEEK I FELT

HOW I WOULD RATE MYSELF THIS WEEK

☆ ☆ ☆ ☆ ☆

The most dangerous people are those who run away from change.

They are also the most energy sucking.

'If I can't trust you, it doesn't matter how smart you are.'

The best advice I have ever got!

Entrepreneurship is not a profession.

It's a state of mind.

There is only one person stopping you from being your own best friend: the person in the mirror.

The world's opinion about us is a reflection of our own opinion about ourselves.

Do not seek distraction from your thoughts by running towards people and things.

My Sunday page

DATE: / /

TOP 3 THINGS I DID THIS WEEK

✓

✓

✓

THE BEST THING THAT HAPPENED TO ME THIS WEEK

WHAT I WANT TO DO NEXT WEEK

THIS WEEK I FELT

HOW I WOULD RATE MYSELF THIS WEEK

Do not make anybody else responsible for your happiness.

The way you respond to the world is the way you teach the world how to treat you.

Good people pay a far higher price for being good than bad people pay for being bad.

Build a team so strong that someone from the outside doesn't know who the boss is!

Entrepreneurship is the most brutal way to discover yourself.

The toughest skill as a leader is to be calm during the toughest moments.

My Sunday page

DATE: /   /

TOP 3 THINGS I DID THIS WEEK

✓

✓

✓

THIS WEEK I FELT

HOW I WOULD RATE MYSELF THIS WEEK

☆ ☆ ☆ ☆ ☆

THE BEST THING THAT HAPPENED TO ME THIS WEEK

WHAT I WANT TO DO NEXT WEEK

Show people who they can be.
Instead of telling them who they shouldn't be.

Every single second you continue to hold on to the time gone by is a second away from shaping your future.

Build a culture that picks people up when they are down.

Our power to imagine is both a strength and a weakness.

If you show to the world your flaws before they point them out, they are left with nothing to troll.

Before you begin to spiral in your own thoughts, ask yourself, 'Would I say this to my best friend?'

My Sunday page

DATE: /   /

TOP 3 THINGS I DID THIS WEEK

✓ ....

....

✓ ....

....

✓ ....

....

THE BEST THING THAT HAPPENED TO ME THIS WEEK

....
....
....
....
....
....

WHAT I WANT TO DO NEXT WEEK

....
....
....
....
....
....
....
....

THIS WEEK I FELT

HOW I WOULD RATE MYSELF THIS WEEK

Only when we shut the door of our ego and be open to learning something new do we realize how much we don't know.

We tend to see the destination as progress. But it is the journey that shows your progress.

The three worst reasons to become an entrepreneur:

1. I want to make money
2. I hate my current job
3. Everyone is doing it

A great leader should be replaceable when it comes to their tasks and actions.

And irreplaceable when it comes to their thoughts and vision.

In a society where being trusted is not common, operating with trust is a competitive advantage. People inherently want to be trusted.

Would you be friends with your own self?
Would you marry yourself?
Would you be your own boss?
What version of you would you rather not be?

Why do you still continue being that version?

You can neither choose your parents nor what they end up doing to you psychologically. Be prepared to heal yourself if you have to.

My Sunday page

DATE: /   /

TOP 3 THINGS I DID THIS WEEK

✓

✓

✓

THE BEST THING THAT HAPPENED TO ME THIS WEEK

WHAT I WANT TO DO NEXT WEEK

THIS WEEK I FELT

HOW I WOULD RATE MYSELF THIS WEEK

☆ ☆ ☆ ☆

Holding a grudge against someone requires a lot of effort. Think of all the wasted time spent being mad at someone.

Every problem in this world can be traced back to a point of miscommunication.

There is a big difference between saying thank you and feeling thankful.

Nothing teaches you better than teaching others.

To start with 'you're right' is great.

To do so in public, when you don't have to is greatness!

Your kindness might cause you pain, a sense of betrayal, heartburn. Be kind anyway.

My Sunday page

DATE: /   /

TOP 3 THINGS I DID THIS WEEK

✓ ....

....

....

✓ ....

....

....

✓ ....

....

....

THIS WEEK I FELT

HOW I WOULD RATE MYSELF THIS WEEK

☆ ☆ ☆ ☆ ☆

THE BEST THING THAT HAPPENED TO ME THIS WEEK

....

....

....

....

....

....

....

WHAT I WANT TO DO NEXT WEEK

....

....

....

....

....

....

....

Unpopular opinion:

Empathy cannot be taught. You are either born with it or not.

Winning is not the purpose of life. To get better at living it, is.

No one is useless.

Everyone knows something you don't.

By not appreciating someone for their vulnerability and truth, all we do is encourage lying.

True respect is when you respect someone even after you've got to know them.

Do not show up for every argument you are invited to!

An undeniable life hack for your peace.

My Sunday page

DATE: /   /

TOP 3 THINGS I DID THIS WEEK

✓

✓

✓

THIS WEEK I FELT

HOW I WOULD RATE MYSELF THIS WEEK

☆ ☆ ☆ ☆ ☆

THE BEST THING THAT HAPPENED TO ME THIS WEEK

WHAT I WANT TO DO NEXT WEEK

Respect doesn't come from the title.

It comes from conduct.

There are people who tell you that you are wrong. There are people that help you see where you are wrong. Guess which ones are more important?

We all accept the love we think we deserve.

We don't have to agree with each other as long as we understand each other.

Who you decide to spend your life with. One of the biggest decisions you will make in your life. Don't take it lightly.

Your parents are first humans. Then parents.

My Sunday page

DATE: / /

TOP 3 THINGS I DID THIS WEEK

✓ ....

THE BEST THING THAT HAPPENED TO ME THIS WEEK

✓ ....

✓ ....

WHAT I WANT TO DO NEXT WEEK

THIS WEEK I FELT

HOW I WOULD RATE MYSELF THIS WEEK

☆ ☆ ☆ ☆ ☆

We create our relationships by what we choose to give.

Whenever someone says, 'You will never know how I am feeling', remind yourself that they are telling you life's most fundamental truth.

Your true friends are those who are TRULY happy for you when you succeed. Be that true friend for others.

Stay away from relationships that suck energy out of you.

If you share because you are expecting something in return, it is not sharing.

It is a transaction!

Wanting to maintain a distance from someone you do not relate to anymore doesn't mean you don't care about them.

It just means you care about the relationship you have with yourself more than the one you have with them.

How we treat others is a reflection of how we treat ourselves.

My Sunday page

DATE: /   /

TOP 3 THINGS I DID THIS WEEK

✓ ....
....
....
....

✓ ....
....
....
....

✓ ....
....
....
....

THIS WEEK I FELT

HOW I WOULD RATE MYSELF THIS WEEK

☆ ☆ ☆ ☆ ☆

THE BEST THING THAT HAPPENED TO ME THIS WEEK

....
....
....
....
....
....
....

WHAT I WANT TO DO NEXT WEEK

....
....
....
....
....
....
....

The worst use of your time is comparing yourself to others.

As a matter of fact, all of us can create as many wins for ourselves instead of waiting for someone else to lose.

We are not the average of the five people we spend the most time with.

We are the average of the five thoughts we spend the most time with.

Instead of having imaginary conversations with others, the way is to have real conversations with yourself.

When we write, we are training our brain to select the most important thought out of all that is inside it.

Being an effective communicator is not so much about speaking English fluently or acting confident. It is simply about understanding the emotions of the person you are communicating with.

My Sunday page

DATE: /   /

TOP 3 THINGS I DID THIS WEEK

✓

✓

✓

THE BEST THING THAT HAPPENED TO ME THIS WEEK

WHAT I WANT TO DO NEXT WEEK

THIS WEEK I FELT

HOW I WOULD RATE MYSELF THIS WEEK

☆ ☆ ☆ ☆

When you spend time with people who are nothing like you, you stretch your fixed mindset to have a wider perspective.

Those with a growth mindset understand risk instead of running away from it.

The mistake most of us make, that keeps us fixed in our mindset, is to believe that we deserve to be where we are in life.

If the decision we take doesn't work out, we can always go back to where we started.

You will never know whether the decision is right or wrong unless you've made it in the first place!

Before you decide on the answer, ask yourself if you have asked all the difficult questions.

My Sunday page

DATE: /   /

TOP 3 THINGS I DID THIS WEEK

✓

✓

✓

THIS WEEK I FELT

HOW I WOULD RATE MYSELF THIS WEEK
☆ ☆ ☆ ☆ ☆

THE BEST THING THAT HAPPENED TO ME THIS WEEK

WHAT I WANT TO DO NEXT WEEK

Wasting your time and letting your mind wander should be a part of your schedule.

You will be able to manage your time only when you understand your relationship with it.

Criticism from our loved ones hurts us because we have put them on a pedestal.

However, true love also means showing the mirror.

All things seem to get better when we look within.

Examine what is said, not who speaks.

Even in our darkest moments, when we think we don't have a choice, we always have a choice.

My Sunday page

DATE: /   /

TOP 3 THINGS I DID THIS WEEK

✓ ....

✓ ....

✓ ....

THIS WEEK I FELT

HOW I WOULD RATE MYSELF THIS WEEK

☆ ☆ ☆ ☆ ☆

THE BEST THING THAT HAPPENED TO ME THIS WEEK

WHAT I WANT TO DO NEXT WEEK

The change we
want in others is
the change we
need to begin with.

The reason most of us do not end up getting wiser is that we worry about looking foolish in front of people who are not even thinking of us!

Meditation does not make you control your emotions.

It instead makes you aware of them.

The purpose of an emotion is not to solve what you are feeling but to make you aware of what you are feeling.

**The best time to plant the tree was yesterday.
The next best time is today.**

Being smart and witty can never compensate for lack of trust. Ever.

When you are accountable to yourself, it doesn't matter who else you are accountable to.

My Sunday page

DATE: /   /

TOP 3 THINGS I DID THIS WEEK

✓

✓

✓

THIS WEEK I FELT

HOW I WOULD RATE MYSELF THIS WEEK

☆ ☆ ☆ ☆

THE BEST THING THAT HAPPENED TO ME THIS WEEK

WHAT I WANT TO DO NEXT WEEK

Of the things that you love doing and are good at, not everything will be something that the world needs or cares about.

Set out to explore careers that nudge you towards them, like a traveller with no destination.

No one should settle down. Keep up that fire. Keep moving the needle.

You weren't born to just settle down!

Life is difficult if you keep proclaiming that it is.

We think some people wake up in the morning wanting to screw up our happiness. But no one cares. Everyone is busy thinking about their own lives.

When we put down our glasses and look at the world through someone else's, we see a different world altogether.

My Sunday page

DATE: /   /

TOP 3 THINGS I DID THIS WEEK

✓ ....

....

....

✓ ....

....

....

✓ ....

....

....

THE BEST THING THAT HAPPENED TO ME THIS WEEK

....

....

....

....

....

....

WHAT I WANT TO DO NEXT WEEK

....

....

....

....

....

....

THIS WEEK I FELT

HOW I WOULD RATE MYSELF THIS WEEK
☆ ☆ ☆ ☆ ☆

If comparison led you to where you wanted to go, people would do nothing other than compare.

We all suffer from this bias, where we think the definition of success is doing the bare minimum. In reality, it is the opposite.

Be nice to people, because you are genuinely nice.

If an impact is all you chase, without being ready for it, you will always settle for much less than you could have achieved.

In a rapidly changing world, the ability to become a student whenever you have to is a superpower!

Listen intently. To opinions and reactions around you.

My Sunday page

DATE: /   /

TOP 3 THINGS I DID THIS WEEK

✓ ....

....

....

✓ ....

....

....

✓ ....

....

....

THE BEST THING THAT HAPPENED TO ME THIS WEEK

WHAT I WANT TO DO NEXT WEEK

THIS WEEK I FELT

HOW I WOULD RATE MYSELF THIS WEEK

☆ ☆ ☆ ☆

If we just do what we are supposed to do, we will just get what we are supposed to get. Not what we desire to get.

Imagine the joy if what you enjoy personally is also what you do professionally.

It's okay to put yourself first. It's absolutely okay to love yourself first because nothing flows out of an empty cup.

With changing times, taking time to reflect isn't a luxury. It is a necessity.

Is there a concept of others in the absence of the self?

Did you know that most people are not aware of what you are going through?

My Sunday page

DATE: /   /

TOP 3 THINGS I DID THIS WEEK

✓ ....
....
....
....

✓ ....
....
....
....

✓ ....
....
....
....

THIS WEEK I FELT

HOW I WOULD RATE MYSELF THIS WEEK

☆ ☆ ☆ ☆ ☆

THE BEST THING THAT HAPPENED TO ME THIS WEEK

....
....
....
....
....
....
....

WHAT I WANT TO DO NEXT WEEK

....
....
....
....
....
....
....

When we disguise our desires as our needs, we almost always end up making a mistake.

Seeking help is the most fundamental way of learning.

Instead of saying no, ask if it's okay to say no? Few will object to that.

Don't start with wanting to convince. Start with wanting to converse.

When nothing else works, there is always help.

True love forgives, even when no apology is sought. Because it can.

Be interested in people. Genuinely interested in people.

My Sunday page

DATE: /   /

TOP 3 THINGS I DID THIS WEEK

✓ ....

✓ ....

✓ ....

THIS WEEK I FELT

HOW I WOULD RATE MYSELF THIS WEEK

☆ ☆ ☆ ☆ ☆

THE BEST THING THAT HAPPENED TO ME THIS WEEK

....

WHAT I WANT TO DO NEXT WEEK

....

To build strong friendships, do not go out desperately looking for friends.

Here is the biggest truth of life – the only best friend you will ever have is yourself.

There is no bigger joy than finding comfort in your own presence.

Having friends is actually wonderful because they allow you to meet a part of you that isn't a part of you.

All friendships boil down to being honest.

You will find a partner when you are not looking for one.

My Sunday page

DATE: /   /

TOP 3 THINGS I DID THIS WEEK

✓ ....
  ....
  ....
  ....

✓ ....
  ....
  ....
  ....

✓ ....
  ....
  ....
  ....

THIS WEEK I FELT

HOW I WOULD RATE MYSELF THIS WEEK
☆ ☆ ☆ ☆

THE BEST THING THAT HAPPENED TO ME THIS WEEK
....
....
....
....
....
....
....
....
....
....

WHAT I WANT TO DO NEXT WEEK
....
....
....
....
....
....
....
....
....

What you do and how do you go about it will change. Why you do things tends to remain constant.

Those who feel complete by themselves make the other person's life better by their presence.

No one can force a relationship on us. Including our own selves.

If you do not acknowledge what you are feeling, the suppression will end up making you angry, resentful and underconfident.

Whatever you are feeling today will eventually fade away.

A happy person will never make you feel unhappy about yourself.

My Sunday page

DATE: / /

TOP 3 THINGS I DID THIS WEEK

✓ ....
....
....
....

✓ ....
....
....
....

✓ ....
....
....
....

THIS WEEK I FELT

HOW I WOULD RATE MYSELF THIS WEEK
☆ ☆ ☆ ☆ ☆

THE BEST THING THAT HAPPENED TO ME THIS WEEK

....
....
....
....
....
....
....

WHAT I WANT TO DO NEXT WEEK

....
....
....
....
....
....
....

Most of us aren't aware of what we want, yet we expect everyone else to respect what we want.

**No one loves adhering to routines.
But everyone LOVES the results routines bring.**

When we set and respect our boundaries, we also encourage others to create and respect theirs.

The toxicity you feel in a relationship is an opportunity to understand your relationship with yourself.

The start of the day is critical to how the rest of the day goes.

Habits are things you do repeatedly so your brain can do them on autopilot.

My Sunday page

DATE: /   /

TOP 3 THINGS I DID THIS WEEK

✓

✓

✓

THE BEST THING THAT HAPPENED TO ME THIS WEEK

WHAT I WANT TO DO NEXT WEEK

THIS WEEK I FELT

HOW I WOULD RATE MYSELF THIS WEEK
☆ ☆ ☆ ☆

Habits that give big results start small. Because they are a consequence of pleasure, not pressure.

Just because you didn't create the problem doesn't mean you don't solve the problem.

Eliminate all distractions that come in the way of you and your new habit.

Unless you know why you do something in the first place, you won't be able to change it.

Anger's purpose is to make us aware of an unresolved need. The moment we become aware of that need, anger has served its purpose.

You feel like a failure because you are not sure of winning again.

My Sunday page

DATE: /   /

TOP 3 THINGS I DID THIS WEEK

✓

✓

✓

THIS WEEK I FELT

HOW I WOULD RATE MYSELF THIS WEEK

☆ ☆ ☆ ☆ ☆

THE BEST THING THAT HAPPENED TO ME THIS WEEK

WHAT I WANT TO DO NEXT WEEK

The strange thing about winning is that it isn't about winning. It is about a feeling of progress.

Attitude compensates for skills. Skills never compensate for attitude.

Instead of reducing expenses, focus on increasing income.

Money is simply a medium of transaction. When it becomes an emotion, that is when it consumes us.

People who are loved the most, are the ones who believe that they are worthy of love.

Who you are and where you came from doesn't matter. What you do and where you are going, is all that does.

My Sunday page

DATE: /   /

TOP 3 THINGS I DID THIS WEEK

✓

✓

✓

THIS WEEK I FELT

HOW I WOULD RATE MYSELF THIS WEEK
☆ ☆ ☆ ☆

THE BEST THING THAT HAPPENED TO ME THIS WEEK

WHAT I WANT TO DO NEXT WEEK